Proving the Impossible

Copyright © 2020 by Santiego Rivers

All rights reserved. No part of this book may be reproduced or transmitted in any form without the written permission of the author.

I choose not to remember parts of my life, but I will never forget because there is no testimony without going through your test.

You will either build or destroy, lose, or win, but the choice is yours either way.

All my life, most people around me had made me feel inferior, which made it easy for me to grasp. I learned to doubt myself before I ever had the confidence to believe in the greatness within me. **(I am H.I.M.)**

It took facing my fears and many tears to learn to ask myself one simple question. Who am I not to be great? In my pursuit of self-discovery, I learned how to stop letting the devil use me because I allowed others to use me for my self-destruction. I was my greatest enemy, which turned out to be a problem that I could fix. All journeys start from the inside. No one can stop a G.O.D. from being a G.O.D., but themselves. **(H.I.M.)**

I had to discover two important things to remove all my doubts & fears, which would stop me from being the best version of myself that I could be. I had questions in my head; Why was I born & what was my purpose in life?

Those unanswered questions filled my mind with a void that became the devil's playground. Those disagreeable beings taught me to hate myself, making it easy for me to hate others and have no remorse for hurting them.

Deep inside, I knew that what I was doing was wrong, but it allowed the victim of so much pain & hurt not to feel like a victim anymore. After years and years of pain, I was ready to lay down all my burdens. You can't truly embrace love if you refuse to let go of the problems holding you back. I had given my pain all that I had to offer; my heart & soul needed love.

I had to learn to eliminate the things and people in my life that didn't help me evolve. The only certainty in life is change. So, if you think you can or you think that you can't, you're right. My pride has always kept me going in the wrong direction in life. It would take all the strength & prayers that I had to surrender to love.

Proving the Impossible
It all started with me

TABLE OF CONTENTS

Putting in That Work 4

As A Man Thinks 6

Turning Your Weaknesses into Your Strengths 8

Finding Your Purpose in Life 10

That Breath of Life 12

Keep Moving Forward 16

What Are You Holding Onto? 19

Skip The "E" And Let It "G.O." 21

Making Sacrifices 23

Discovering the Best Version of Yourself 25

Removing Obstacles 27

Success Is Not for Everyone 29

Becoming the Best Version of You 31

Your Dream Is Not Dead. (It May Not Just Be Your Season) 34

Their Habits, Fears, And Other People's Opinions 35

Your Weaknesses and Your Childish Ways 36

Will You Decide to Go After Your Dreams? 38

Time Waits For No One 40

When It Is All Said and Done (What Will Be Your Final Message) I Came, I Saw, I Conquered 42

Putting in That Work

Putting in that work meant taking ownership of the choices and decisions when it came to my life. If I were going to take the credit for all the good things that happen in my life, I needed to take ownership of how I handled the tests that life blessed me with.

Every trial and tribulation that life brings our way is truly a blessing because it allows us to show our ability to overcome any setback or momentary situation. Life is composed of seconds in minutes, minutes within an hour, and hours within a day. Why should we let a moment in our day affect our whole day?

I am not trying to minimize the bad things that could happen in our life. I am just trying to encourage you to realize that those moments in your life can be the testimony you come to share with someone in need.

There is someone in need of assurance that they are not alone. There is someone who needs to know that there is a light/life at the end of the tunnel. You can be the voice that assures them that the long and hard path that they travel to make it through their storms is worth it.

Those people now smile when the rain begins to fall because they know that this downpour of rain will produce a rainbow when it finishes. These are the people who have learned to understand that they are stronger than any situation that life will bring their way.

You being stronger does not mean that you will not be hurt or disappointed when you face challenging times. You realize that hard times don't last, but tough people do. The secret to tough people is their ability to keep getting up. Tough people are willing to put in that work.

If you don't like the current situation that you are facing, why not change it? I am not saying that change will occur overnight. I am just saying to start working on a plan to change your current situation. The first thing you must change is your way of thinking.

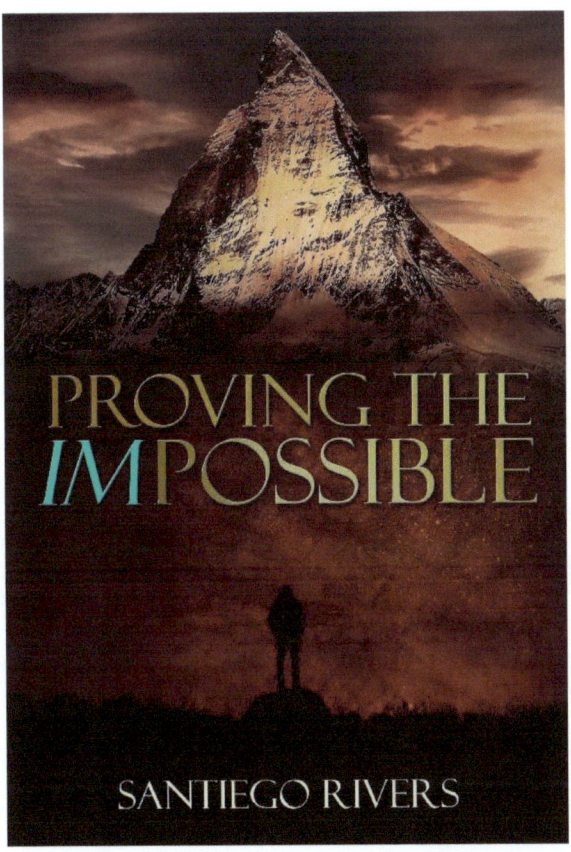

As A Man Thinks....

Are you an elephant or a lion? The difference between an elephant and a Lion is the mindset. The elephant is the hunted, and the lion is the hunter simply because of their thinking.

The greatest obstacle/nemesis to a person is the mind and its negative thoughts. There is no prison worse than the prison of the mind. My wife suffers from diagnosed **P.T.S.D.** Together we go through many troubling days, and it is a constant battle that one day we will claim victory over.

Victory is the outcome that drives people with a positive mindset. When failure is not an option, you find ways to make success possible. Victory becomes possible when you understand that **F.A.I.L.** only stands for your **First Attempt in Learning.**

Failure only occurs when you stop trying to succeed. When I first went to college, I did not graduate. I thought that I would never earn my college degree. I just assumed that I had missed that opportunity. Fifteen years later, I received my college degree and had the job I dreamed of as a child. I became a Certified Teacher.

Once I stopped my negative thinking and started applying myself, I started accomplishing small victories that soon became significant triumphs in my life. Every journey begins with a tiny step. My beginning started with going back to school.

I asked myself one simple question; why not? I knew that women did it all the time, so why would I let my pride stop me from accomplishing one of my dreams? I have always liked school and learning new things. So, why not go back to school and better my life and my family life as well?

I will admit that my journey was not comfortable, but luckily, I am a very stubborn person. I positively used my stubbornness, and I did not give up.

Turning Your Weaknesses into Your Strengths

Procrastinating / Being Stubborn / Being late /

These are a few of the things I have inherited from both of my parents. I will also mention that I have inherited some great qualities, as well. Learning to overcome/turn my shortcomings into a positive thing has been a challenge that did not come easy.

The hardest part about overcoming any challenge is dealing with yourself. Change and acceptance do not come easy. The only thing that comes easy in life is failure / quitting. It doesn't require any effort. Losing or quitting was never an option, so I struggled to succeed, but I did.

Procrastinating is something I still must be mindful of today, even as an adult. I know that I find it hard to get back to doing it if I put something off. Therefore, I try my best to complete tasks right away.

I often find myself juggling two to three tasks at a time in a workday. The way my mind works, doing multiple tasks allow me to have peace of mind, strange as it may seem. Now that I'm older and conscious of my shortcomings, my mind does not allow me to rest if I don't complete major tasks by a specific time. There are still those <u>*honey-to-do list*</u> things I will eventually get to finish.

Being Stubborn is not a bad thing if you learn to use it positively. Be stubborn when it comes to not giving up, settling for less than what you work hard for, and not being the best person, you can be.

I dislike being late; my new motto is that if you are not early, you are late. As a child, my mom, bless her soul, often made me late for school and other activities I had to attend. As an adult, I still have nightmares about being late to work or any event. I would always set my alarm clock early because I knew that I am not a morning person, and it took time for me to get up. Now, I wake up without an alarm clock because I have a purpose.

Finding Your Purpose in Life

The greatness of tomorrow starts with the plans and decisions that we make today. Will that dreamer learns to manifest their dream into reality? Will that dreamer know to dream before the doubts of others become the thoughts that are the loudest in the dreamer's mind? **(Please read again for clarity)**

Often in our lives, we deal with people who don't believe in us or share our vision. Those situations are painful feelings from the people we depend on or want to have our back as we embark on our new journey.

Over time, this may lead to us having self-doubt and question the path that we are on. Over time, I learned that no person could stop what the Most High has planned for you in life. Only you can fall short of fulfilling your real purpose in life by the decisions you make today.

Each decision has its consequences. Some of the results are good, and some of them let us know that we need to make some changes in our life. Transitions are the only certainty in life. The question you need to ask yourself is, are you going to do it willingly, or will you continue to fight the inevitable?

I never took the straight path anywhere in my life. Obstacles filled my whole life with many detours and side roads before I learned to stop and formulate a plan. Before I had my goal, I needed to find my purpose for traveling the road ahead.

My purpose in life is to be a servant to others. I am happiest when I can aid/assist someone on their path. I have discovered that only when I stop doing what I was designed to do, I begin to struggle in life.

When your work fits with your purpose, it's like you are not working. Every morning, I wake up happy because I plan to connect with someone I can help. I firmly believe that you should do the following to be happy truly:

Live a life worth remembering so that your good deeds will speak life to those who desperately need a breath of life.

That Breath of Life

Your words can be the breath of life to someone, or your comments can be the demise of their spirit that kills their flesh. As a child, the person who was supposed to make me feel that my life mattered gave me reasons to hate myself, making it easy for me to hate others because I was in so much pain.

For years I struggled with insecurities, anger, and hate because I felt unloved. These feelings have haunted me even as I became an adult. I failed with long-term relationships and being close to others simply because I felt so undeserving. My insecure feelings made me search for acceptance from situations and people that did not have my best interest in mind. When you don't get that breath of life from the people that you need it from, you then accept it in any way that you can get it.

I Love You / You are Special / You are Handsome or Beautiful

These simple words I struggled to tell my children growing up because I never heard or was showed as a child enough. There are many lessons that I did not receive as a child that I am still trying to learn as an adult.

If feeling loved was oxygen, I felt that I was always short of breath. I bounced from home to home within my family, searching for love & a sense of belonging. I carried these same faults into the relationships I had as an adult.

My wife will tell you that I will leave her in a second because of the jagged pieces I am still trying to smooth out. I love my wife with all my heart, but I will walk out the door in a second because I am damaged goods. I am still and always going to

Be a work in progress. Being with my wife is the longest stable relationship that I have ever endured. She has given me a reason not to want to pack my bags and leave. My wife has given me a real family and the opportunity to raise our daughter together under one roof. **(Pray for Us)** I want this to work.

I no longer blame that person who made me feel the way that I did as a child. I understand that we often imitate what happened to us as a child when we become an adult. Damaged goods often produce damaged goods. It takes the following to break the cycle created by being damaged goods.

Hard Work / Sacrifice / Faith / Determination / Struggle / Failure / Patience It all starts with you

The easiest thing to do is blame others for all the wrongs in our lives and take full credit for all the good things that happen to us. These are ways of a selfish person.

I feel that this would be the understanding of a fool and his thoughts as well. A fool believes that If it weren't for the flaws in the stars', the sky would be so beautiful, but it takes a wise person to realize that it is the flaws that make everything attractive.

A diamond is priceless based upon its flaws

Blaming others for all the wrong choices/decisions that we make in life makes us a fool. Learning that the decision to react negatively is our choice which puts us on the right path to enlightenment.

When it comes to the fool and the wise man, the question is simple for the wise man. The choices and the decisions that you are making in your life; how is the outcome working for you?

I'm not talking about how it is working out for the people you blame for your demise; I'm talking about you. While you are holding onto all that anger inside and losing sleep at night, your nemesis is happy and sleeping well at night. Your emotions are keeping you up. **(How's it working for you)**

A fool sees other people as their greatest enemy, but a wise person realizes that their anger & pride are their greatest nemesis that they must learn to overcome. The path to success contains the bricks of the following:

Hard Work / Sacrifice / Faith / Determination / Struggle / Failure / Patience

It's going to take **hard work** to put your ability to think before the emotions of your anger & pride. You will have to **sacrifice** your feelings to truly nourish your ability to think and make the best decisions for yourself.

You will have to have **faith** and trust the process because there will be many times where doubt will set in. You must be determined to succeed and see this journey through. The road to success is long, but it is indeed worth it. Your anger & your pride will cause you to struggle because they will give life to your doubt, and if you give in, you will surely fail.

You are going to have to learn to trust the process that leads to the needed change. This change will require **patience** and understanding. There will be many setbacks, but it is okay if you stay on the path. **(keep moving forward)**

The bridge between your dreams and reality is hard work. Working hard in life helps bring your dreams closer to reality. The only question you need to ask yourself is," How bad do you want it?" Success does a great job of weeding out the weak. **(Think about that)**

Each morning before you start your day, in your mind, set the tone of your day for victory!!! Don't put anything before your success.

Being lazy, being tired, other people's opinions of you. You must develop the mindset that says, **"I don't care if you don't like me because I love myself!"**

Raise your living standards, and you will significantly increase your altitude as you shoot for the stars. Keep moving in the direction of success.

Keep Moving Forward

Life will present you with many reasons to stop moving forward on your path to greatness. You need to be **_too damn stubborn_** and determined to reach your destiny, to quit.

To keep moving forward in the face of adversity is a skill set learned going through trials and tribulations. You can teach a person how to respond during tough times, but that will never guarantee success when that moment comes if they have not been through the fire.

Every small challenge in life prepares us for the great tests life will eventually bring our way. There's an old saying that states. *"Tough times don't last, but tough people do."*

I have faced many challenges in my life that would have broken lesser men, but I am still here. I have fallen numerous times, but I have refused to stay down. It's not over until I win.

Yes, most of my setbacks were very hard to deal with in life. I remembered from my earlier tests in life that all things are possible because I am.

In my mind, nothing is impossible. I'm in the word impossible because I am possible. My prayers, my faith, and my work make all things possible in my life. I have dwelt in the valley of woe, but my mind, my dedication, and my work effort would not allow me to accept that at the bottom is where I belonged.

Where I belong is the place where the Most High created me to dwell. My place is on a high, next to the throne. The ability to think, say & do is what keeps me healthy. When you learn who you are, then you know how to act. **(I am H.I.M)**

Think / Say / Do

Words have the power to change lives. What you think becomes what you say; what you say becomes what you do. So, why not think, say, and do things to make your life better?

Having a better life is a choice that only you can make. You control your destiny. How you react to the tests that life brings your way is totally on you. Every obstacle that you face in life is only a test to see how you will respond to adversity.

Facing adversity tells the real character of a person. Will you remain calm when the temperature gets hot, or will you boil over like boiling water? What you think & say does not always translate to what you do at that moment. Therefore, every life test has a purpose for your future.

Our lives have daily tests/obstacles that should prepare us for the real challenges that life will bring our way. Will you learn to smile amid adversity?

Why is it important to learn to smile at the beginning of any trials that you may face? A smile allows your body to relax and focus. Life is a game of chess, not checkers. Every move in your life should be thoroughly thought out and have a purpose. Every action comes with consequences.

Our emotions do not change the choices we must make. Our feelings often lead to us making worse long-term decisions. You may be upset today, but tomorrow or in the future, what happens when you think back on that situation with a clearer mind? There are no *"do-overs"* in life.

Your thoughts become the words that you say, which becomes the things that you do. Disagreeable thoughts become bad words that become evil actions. Good ideas become kind words that become agreeable actions.

Life will present you with many tests. You will have many opportunities to learn and grow from each situation. Never give up because you only fail when you decide to stop trying. Think positive thoughts because they will lead to you saying encouraging words and doing beautiful things.

What Are You Holding Onto?

Your past should never define you. It is your actions today which will determine your future. A diamond comes from coal. A mustard seed grows from dirt. So, why can't you be like a phoenix and rise from the ashes?

It takes hitting rock bottom to discover the authentic version of yourself. Anyone can shine from the top of the mountain, but can you withstand the woes you will face in the valley?

You will encounter many people blaming others in the valley because they are not on the top of the mountain. While looking for sympathy amongst the bucket of crabs, the people with focus and purpose are planning their path back to the mountain top.

How will you get to the top of your mountain? Will your emotions and anger put a halt on your journey? You hold the answer to both questions, but you must release both things to climb.
Hates begets hate, pain produces suffering, but only learning to forgive releases you from both crutches. Will you rise or fall? Will you win or lose? Only you can determine the outcome.

The tighter you hold onto anything, the more you will stop your progress in life. On your climb to the top of the mountain, you are continuously moving and changing your grip. Once you stop doing these things, you are stuck where you are. The key to the climb is to grab and release. This skill set translates to our daily life. Don't get stuck holding onto any emotions that don't inspire you to keep moving forward. Onward & upwards is the path.

After all your grabbing and releasing, you will eventually reach the top of your mountain. Only then will you discover that there is no mountain. There is only a place for you to ascend to greater heights. You have only reached your launching pad for your next challenge.

You can't ascend by holding onto things; you must become light as a feather and let go of everything that stops you from rising. It would be best if you learned to take your ego out of the equation. This hindrance is one weight that will make it very hard for you to climb.

The truth is that everything you will need to succeed is already at your fingertips.

Skip The "E" And Let It "G.O." …

Your *E.G.O.* will be the demise of you. Your *E.G.O.* will be the demise of your future. My uncle told me that the word E.G.O. stands for *Edging God Out*.

The word E.G.O. can stand for *Edging Goodness Out* if you are not a religious person.

I don't want a specific word to stop you from getting the message because the most crucial part is that you get the message.

> The message is: **don't let your ego make your journey to your self-discovery harder than what it will already be**.

You will have other disagreeable beings putting up roadblocks to your success along the way. They do not need your help. Your anger, stubbornness & pride are worse than any obstacle that the enemy can use to halt your journey.

Your anger, your stubbornness, and your pride are a sure way to push the Most High out of your life. Goodness does not dwell where evil is. Evil is considered the absents of good. You see the rainbow after the storm is over, not during the storm.

All you must do to make your journey to self-discovery more accessible is to put down your burdens/ego and open your heart to love.

Holding onto hatred makes it hard for you to open your heart and let love into your soul. I am a firm believer that you need to skip the **"E"** and let everything in your life that does not serve the purpose of making you happy **"G.O."**

Let it go for your happiness. Let it go for your peace of mind. You must be tired of always being sick and tired of going through the same thing every day?

Some people often define insanity as doing the same thing repeatedly and expecting a different outcome. You change your clothes every day, so why not change your way of thinking and doing in the same manner?

You are going to have to make some sacrifices in life to win the game of life.

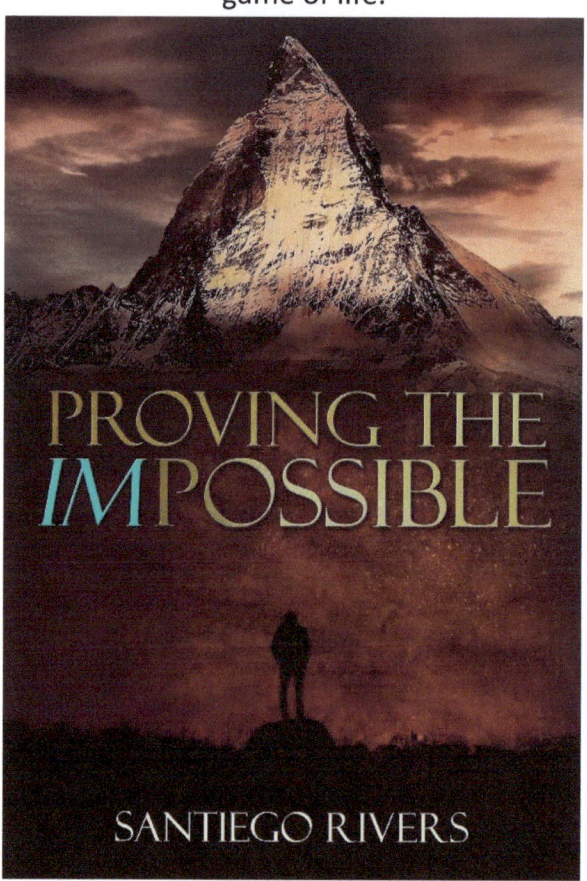

Making Sacrifices

I am sure that we have all heard the old saying that you can't always have your cake and eat it too.

As a child, that never really made sense to me. I will admit that I fight against that even as an adult. Who wants to make tough sacrifices in life? Why can't it just be easy?

As a child, I wanted money, but I didn't want to work for it. As a child, I wanted nice things, but I did not want to take care of them the way I should. That part didn't apply to me because I didn't like people playing with my toys. After all, they might have broken them. I think you get my point?

As an adult, my ego & pride made it easy for me to walk away from jobs and people and do what I dreamed of doing in life. My mentality was, *"Fuck It and You."*

As a child, I was never taught or made to work out my problems and see them through. Remember earlier that I told you that I came from broken parents who raised a broken child. I had many destructive internal issues/conflicts that I never worked out in my youth. I apologize to those who had to deal with the adult version of me still working out my childhood problems.

It took making many mistakes to finally realize that the way I was doing things in my life was not working out for me and my well-being. I had to look in the mirror and ask myself the question, *"How is it working out for you"*?

Self-reflection is a humbling thing, but it is indeed worth it. I find it better to learn how to check yourself than to have others point out your character flaws repeatedly.

A child must sacrifice his childish ways to become an adult. An adult must learn how to resolve his selfish desires to learn how to become the best version of themselves. It is not easy, but you will find out that it is worth it in the end.

Who will you discover when you discover the best version of yourself?

Discovering the Best Version of Yourself

As a child, I dreamed that I was a superhero, but I always woke up a mere mortal being. Why did I have dreams that I was powerful beyond the limitations of my doubts and fears? Why did I let the words of others haunt me for so many years?

For so many years, I ignored my dreams because I always have awoken to my reality. My reality was that I felt like I wasn't shit, far too often in my life. Too many times, my mother told me that I was stupid.
How could I be superman when the people around me made me feel less than Clark Kent?

Fortunately for me, I had a few people in my life that nurtured a boy's dreams until that adult would have the courage to turn those dreams into reality. It took years to discover how to be the best version of myself, and it is still a work in progress.

I still have those inner doubts, but the work that I put in to keep pushing towards my self-discovery and my real purpose in life drown any doubt.

I learned that my dreams of greatness were a glimpse into my life if I made the sacrifices and put in the work it took to achieve my destiny.

I learned that your feet could never take you to any place that your mind has not already envisioned. My mind reminded me of my real purpose and my God-given gifts, even when I let my doubts and the words of others deem my light.

When I discovered the best version of myself and my purpose in life, it allowed me to lay down all my burdens, doubts, and fears of being who I was to become. I am a sensitive, caring, loving soul who is not perfect, but I am excellent in my effort. I enjoy helping others and trying to make the world around me a better place.

To be the best version of myself, I had to remove the people and the things out of my life that did not support my growth. Removing certain people and things from my inner circle was one of those tough sacrifices.

Removing Obstacles

Whatever obstacles you place in your way, you have the power to remove them. Removing barriers and people from your life does not mean you are a cold-hearted person; it only means that you are in the pursuit of your self-discovery.

When it comes to people who genuinely love you, they will help guide you on your path. They will be your guide, your sounding board, even your motivation to keep moving forward when you want to stop.

I have stopped moving forward many times on my journey because I made the road hard for myself. I placed obstacles and roadblocks in my path. I let people steer me off course because I was afraid to travel alone.

It took many, many, many years to learn that rather I succeed or fail was totally on me. I had to be selfish and stubborn about reaching my goals in life. My mother had her life to live. My father had his life to live. I had to live my life. You can't please everybody, so why not make yourself happy?

I had to find the things that made me smile and gave my life purpose. Pleasing other people did not make me happy. I have always danced to the rhythm of my music. I find it hard to fit in. I only know how to stand out. **(Sorry that I'm not sorry)**

The main obstacle in my life was trying to fit into the mold that other people wanted me to be. I learned that I could only be me. Now I was ready to proceed on my journey.

It takes clarity to see the path before you on your journey. Life is a game of chess, not checkers. You must learn to see moves ahead, or you will continuously fall into many traps in life.

Success Is Not for Everyone

Everybody wants success, but not everybody is willing to put in that work. You can't dream yourself into success. Reaching success in your life requires making the right moves in your life.

People who are successful in life learns the importance of taking ownership of their words, thoughts, and actions. No one will get up early in the morning and do the road work to improve your stamina. No one will put up 1000 shots a day to enhance your shooting ability for you. No one will go to the classroom to do your work to make you eligible to play sports.

Your success depends on you and the effort that you are willing to put forward. Successful people have many setbacks in life. Thomas Edison failed in perfecting the light bulb many times before he finally got it right. All these people knew one crucial thing when it came to success. You only must get it right one time to achieve success in anything.

For most people, quitting is more comfortable than trying. It takes making yourself uncomfortable in life to see and make a real change in your life. **(let me repeat it)** It takes making yourself uncomfortable in life to see and make a fundamental change in your life. You must learn to be comfortable being uncomfortable

Your path to success is designed for you by the Most High. The only thing you must do is take that first step, and The Most High will lead the way. Will you start your journey or find reasons why you will not put forth any effort?

Your scars, your bruises, and all the naysayers in your life serve a purpose. They are put in your life to help you develop the character to help make your success that much better when you have achieved it.

If you put forth the work, you will achieve success. You may not be a millionaire or the next Lebron James. You will achieve success by becoming the best version of yourself!!!

Becoming the Best Version of You

I used to be everything that I now hate in a man, but I have changed. **(Let me repeat this)** I used to be everything that I now despise in a man, but I have changed.

People in your life will not accept you now as the person you have developed to because they have not changed. Their way of thinking is this," Who are you to become somebody because I still feel like I am a nobody?"

Don't let anybody tie you to the person you were because they can't accept the person you are today. As an infant grows into a child and a child grows into adolescence; You can grow mentally and spiritually to become the best version of yourself. Your hard work, sacrifice, faith, determination, struggle, failure, and patience will produce greatness if you put forth the work required.

It takes work to produce the change that you want and the change that you need. I had to put in that work to change my life in a way that made me happy. I have disappointed many people, including myself, throughout my life. Out of all those people, it was only one person that I had to get right with. **(Myself)**

I had to be accountable to myself. I had to look myself in the mirror and apologize to myself for not living up to the expectations that I have for myself. I did not always put in that needed work. I didn't always come out of my comfort zone to produce the required change. I was afraid of success and becoming the best version of myself simply because I was scared to fail.

Being afraid to fail is the reason many people don't try. You can make many excuses for your lack of effort, but it is out of fear that the elephant is hunted, and the lion is the hunter.

Stop viewing failing and losing as a bad thing. I told you earlier that the word **'F.A.I.L"** stands for your *'First Attempt in Learning."* Make **"L"** stand for a lesson and not a loss.

Making "L" stand for a lesson and not loss...

How do you know how you will perform under pressure if you have not overcome challenges in life? Life is full of lessons that will prepare you for your most challenging battles. There will be some victories and some setbacks, but what you should never encounter are defeats.

Defeats are for those who have given up. Keep fighting! We all must learn when and how to pause or break whenever we are facing a tough battle. I often use the "Serenity Prayer" to understand that I will not always win every battle in that exact moment, but I will fight. **(Serenity/Courage & Wisdom)**

I must understand that everything is not always in my control to change. I should only focus on the things that I can change. I need to learn the difference between the things in my power and the things that are not.

I control my reactions. How I respond to any situation is in my control. Instead of going back and forth with someone, I can simply be quiet. Instead of trying to go through the brick wall, I can simply find another path. Doing these things are not considered a defeat in life. Doing these things does not mean that I have given up on my goals and dreams. Doing these things means that I am simply now focused on my goals and dreams.

Loses are only for those who have given up and refuses to fight. You must fight for what you want in life. The battle will be challenging, but the victory will be worth it. You must learn how to get comfortable being uncomfortable.

Your comfort zone will "Never" put you on the path of success. Your comfort zone will not help make your dreams come true. Just because your dreams don't come true when you want them, it does not mean that they will not manifest when you need them. Goals become a reality when faith and hard work meets and refuses to compromise for anything.

Only the Most High knows your winning season, so in the meantime, keep putting in that work and have faith that your season is coming.

Your Dream Is Not Dead.
(It May Not Just Be Your Season)

If you always do what you have done continuously in life, you will still be in the same place you are currently at in your life. Being comfortable is a cage. All your doubts and fears created that jail or prison that your mind has manifested for you.

You could've, would've, and should've turned into the reasons why you are currently at your present location in life doing nothing productive. You will never change what you have grown to tolerate. You must learn to train your mind to think positively.

You will learn to be productive with your actions. If the thought of your future scares you, that means that you are not ready to turn your dreams into reality.

Most people are governed by the following simply because they don't want to let go:

Their Habits, Fears, And Other People's Opinions

What you say becomes what you do in life. Your fears come from the doubts and opinions of others around you about your future. Just like the seasons comes and go, learn to let go of everything in your life that does not serve the purpose of growth.

Eliminate what does not help you to evolve. Eliminate who you are, not to discover who you were meant to be. Please don't allow your dreams to die because you don't dare to fight for them. Put yourself in a position where you can't retreat, and you will be amazed at the outcome. Do the things that you don't want to do because: On the other side is greatness. All you can do is all you can do. **(Make sure it is enough)**

Learn balance. & develop patience in life. Please, don't rush the process with either step. You may know everything, but the test is putting it into practice. Experience removes all your weaknesses and childish ways.

Your Weaknesses and Your Childish Ways

What is the primary purpose of this book? What do every word and every line written in this book mean? The answer to that question is straightforward. _It is easier to build stronger children than to repair broken adults_.

Adults find it harder to change because they become set in their ways. On the other hand, children can make their weaknesses stronger and get rid of their childish ways because they have not become set in their ways too long. You can still reach children; adults, on the other hand, can be a lot more complicated.

The inability to adapt and change is a weakness that stops growth. The failure to seek growth limits your growth. Yes, everything in your life is connected in one way or another. You must look at yourself in the mirror and speak life into your soul.

Decide/commit/ act /succeed/ repeat

Decide what you want out of life and **commit** to it with all you might. **Act** like there is no option other than to **succeed**. Failure is not an option. When these steps in your life become a reality, **repeat** the process.

Once you grasp this concept, you understand how each step in your life can lead you to the next opportunity to grow. The mind controls the body; it's not the other way around. The lion hunts and the elephant become the hunted because of its' mindset.

It's your attitude that will either propel you to greatness or be the reason that your life is filled with so much regret. Are you the hunter or the hunted? Are you going to be food or the hunter? Only you can decide what your role will be. Your weakness and childish ways will manifest your future.

Get out of your feelings because your feelings are a weakness that will put you on a first-class trip to failure. Put away your childish ways because while you are playing the game of life, the life that you truly desire is getting further away from your grasp.

Will You Decide to Go After Your Dreams?

Don't accept how your life is; decide to change your life by any means necessary. If life is what you make it, why not make your life beautiful? It's going to take some hard work, sacrifice, and many setbacks to make your ordinary life extraordinary by your standards.

Just like failure is a choice, success is also a choice. Will you wake up each morning with a purpose? Will you set daily goals? Will you create that vision board of the things that you want out of life? Will you refuse to settle for anything less than success?

Will you decide to go after your dreams?

The answer to every question begins and ends with you. You are the alpha and the omega when it comes to putting in that work to manifest your dreams into reality. You are the supervisor who decides when the day is over and when the next day begins. You have the only opinion that matters when it comes to your life and your future.

Let your voice be the sound that lifts your mind, body, and soul to new heights. You are all that is needed to achieve success in your life.

Some days in the pursuit of your destiny, you will win. On other days in the pursuit of your dreams, you will encounter some setbacks. Regardless of the setbacks, you must be relentless and stubborn not to stay down for the count.

Fight/fight/fight

And when you are tired and don't think you can carry on, fight, fight, fight some more. *Fight* to overcome your weaknesses. *Fight* to overcome those setbacks. *Fight* because you are too afraid not to give it your all when chasing your dreams.

The dreams that you are unsure of how bad you want, somebody is putting it on their vision board and planning on doing everything you will not so that they can remove that dream from their vision board into their reality.

Time waits for no one

Time Waits For No One

While you sit around waiting for tomorrow to execute your master plan; Tomorrow has quickly become today, and you are a day behind. Time is the illusion that "the have nots" wait for while "they have" controls. **(Let me repeat)** Time is the illusion that "the have nots" wait for while "they have" controls.)

Understanding time may shed light on that old saying that the "Early bird gets the worm." While you are still sleeping, the person who is chasing your same dream is getting closer to their destination. Your goal will no longer be yours because someone else will have already claimed it before your eyes are even open.

Time is not on your side. Time has been working against you from the moment you came out of the womb. You should have told the doctor to find your clothes when you were born because you" Got Shit to Do!"

Make moves in your life today like there is no tomorrow.
Learn to be *a 24-hr person*, and you will live a life that is worth remembering.

You must strive to be better today than yesterday, and tomorrow repeat the same thinking way. There is no room for excuses simply because you do not have time.

Nobody cares about how hard your journey was to success. The only thing that matters in life is you reaching your destination. Life is not a game of horseshoes. Life is a chess game with thought-out moves and strategies to victory that do not consider winning by coming close to success.

Kill or be killed, win or lose; If you did not come to claim victory, then why did you bother to come in the first place? The road to success will always be under construction and have numerous traffic jams.

It will be up to you to find that alternate route because, as I stated earlier," time waits for no one!"

When It Is All Said and Done
(What Will Be Your Final Message)
I Came, I Saw, I Conquered

One day, all your hard work, effort, tears, and patience will pay off. One day, your season of victory will be today. One day, you will be able to look in the mirror and say to yourself, *"Job Well Done,"* as you prepare for the ongoing battle.

When it is all said and done for one goal, it becomes time to remove that goal from your vision board and put up another plan. You must develop the mindset of a conqueror.

Your victory; should give you the confidence to face an even more significant life challenge with each new accomplishment. Each success becomes the next step in achieving your goal in life.

You want to face each new challenge with the following mentality:

I came, I saw, I conquered, Repeat

The conqueror knows that the adversity in life is temporary, but the glory is eternal. Never allow a temporary situation to affect the bigger picture in your life. Let your victories, your resilience, and your determination be the real blueprint when it comes to your life.

Don't allow the doubts, fears, and others' opinions to hinder your path to your success. When it is all said and done, the victory or defeat is yours to claim. So, what will be your final message? What will your actions have to say about the effort that you put forward?

I know what mine will say. I will wait until you publish your book/ testimony to see what you would say.

It Seems Impossible Until it's done

www.ingramcontent.com/pod-product-compliance
Lightning Source LLC
Chambersburg PA
CBHW042329150426
43193CB00005B/61